Nourishing the Spiritual Life

Paul A. Lacey

Quaker Home Service, London

First published March 1995
This edition January 1999
by
QUAKER HOME SERVICE

ISBN 0 85245 309 4

Copy editor: Elisabeth Alley
Design and layout: Jonathan Sargent
Typeface: Bembo, text 12/15pt
Printed in Friends House, London

The Publisher gratefully acknowledges permission to
reproduce the quotations from the poetry of Denise
Levertov in *Breathing the Water*. Copyright Denise Levertov
1987. Reprinted by permission of New Directions
Publishing Corporation. Also to Messrs Faber and Faber
for permission to quote two lines from *Four Quartets* by
T S Eliot. We have tried to obtain permissions regarding all
other quotes in this books. Where this has not been possible,
we are none the less grateful, and will gladly give full
acknowledgements in any future edition.

Contents

The Need for Nourishment

It might be useful, if it were not so frightening, to ask how many people sitting in any particular meeting for worship find themselves in a dry period, getting nothing but a little peace and quiet from the silence and virtually nothing from the spoken ministry. I would hazard the guess that a fair number of people in meeting on any given day would say that they had not much sense of anything happening in their spiritual lives but were in a time of low energy.

As individuals, and as a society, literally and metaphorically, we are malnourished. We are also, to invent a word, 'mal-nurtured', for we are neither tender nor wise in the habits of nourishment we practise.

Metaphorical meanings derive their power from the resonance of literal meanings, the down-to-earth physicality of human life. That is why I find it especially useful, when thinking of the needs of the spiritual life, to anchor my understanding in something as fundamental as feeding.

The over-arching questions of the spiritual life might be put this way: how and what can I be fed, for my best strength, my greatest health, my fullest happiness? What must I learn about my needs, about the world I live in, about other people, which will help me know and practise the habits which bring me strength, health and happiness? Those questions may sound too self-centred, too concerned with my needs in a world where, through no fault of their own, millions of people are chronically unfed, unhealthy, unhappy, unempowered. But a key to living the spiritual life is that we deepen it not only in order to enjoy its benefits but to share what we have found. One way that true spiritual nourishment is unlike food and water, and like learning, is that it is not used up or consumed as we receive it. For me to have spiritual nourishment will not deny it to anyone else but may in fact make it more likely that all of us are better nourished.

Working Definitions

Spiritual: Often the words 'spiritual' and 'spirituality' are used in contrast or opposition to some other term. It is a long tradition, found in the influence of Greek thought on Christianity as well as in eastern religions, to oppose the spiritual to the carnal. 'The spirit is willing, but the flesh is weak.' Often, spiritual will be contrasted to religious or pietistic, words which point to something too restrictive, too dependent on opinions, loyalties to denominations or to what early Friends would have called notions about religion. For many people, especially in contemporary society, religion is what has divided people. It is often associated with dependence on creeds, doctrines, different ways of using language. Piety stresses an over-scrupulous obedience to rules of conduct demanded by a community or a priesthood.

Although early Friends would use traditional Christian language which contrasted spirit with flesh, as in George Fox's refusing to accept a military commission because he knew the cause of wars, 'the lusts of the flesh' as the General Epistle of James expressed it, that contrast never became the basis for otherworldliness. For them, as for us, the spiritual life was to be lived in and through the flesh, finding appropriate expression in political and social action, in the institutions we create. For Friends, nothing could be less spiritual than to allow bodily harm, physical or other oppression to God's children, on the excuse that spirituality is only concerned with some higher reality in which what happens to the body or the emotions is unimportant. Bodily hunger is a spiritual problem precisely because it is a physical, a social and a political problem.

Likewise with the pietism of rules. When Paul of Tarsus says to the Colossians, 'Why let people dictate to you: "Do not handle this, do not taste that, do not touch the other"...?' he is appealing to spiritual knowledge as more dependable, deeper, freer, than following the law. For Paul, as for early Friends and for the majority of Friends in the world today, the knowledge which freed us from the law was the knowledge of Christ in our lives. The Religious Society of Friends shows us how to embrace the spiritual instead of what may become the empty forms of religious observance or piety, but it also shows that embracing the spiritual is something other than radical individualism and idolising personal impulse – the mistakes which characterise the behaviour of ranters, who hide their excesses behind the language of spirituality.

Material prepared for a World Council of Churches assembly, on the theme *Come Holy Spirit: Renew the Whole Creation*, notes:

The Spirit is the women's movement's primary designation for God and the presence of God; and it is no accident that women's spirituality brings together an emphasis on the Spirit and an active concern for reweaving the web of life... Christians engaged with issues of the planetary environment speak of the divine Spirit experienced in creation. The Spirit is the common ground in inter-religious dialogue with other world faiths and the faiths of indigenous peoples.

The World Council of Churches material further comments that the Spirit is also the living force in Pentecostal and Charismatic movements, in Evangelical traditions, conservative and radical, and in the Orthodox tradition. 'It is a promising and widely shared voice of a lively pluralism around the world.'

Like any powerful term in human languages, spiritual can come to mean almost anything good, then almost anything, and finally almost nothing. Spirit is a powerful metaphor, but every metaphor tells only part of the truth. Every metaphor misrepresents or omits something in order to tell its truth. The Spirit may indeed be the common ground for many religious communions, but surely listening to one another with respect and understanding will show how different the human experiences are, for which the single word stands as sign . Shelley reminds us that 'the deep truth is imageless', but humans can only tell the truth of their lives to one another through images, figures and metaphors.

What I believe is the heart of the spiritual life will become clear, I hope, as I describe some of the ways I find it best nourished and nurtured in me. But as a starting point, and with full awareness of how inadequate words are for the task, I offer a brief working definition: I take the spiritual life to be a life which aims to discover human wholeness, the integration of all aspects of our humanity – body, soul, mind, emotions – and the connection of the self to all of creation. As I understand it, the spiritual life is marked by vigorous activity in the world, on behalf of God's creation, in obedience to God's leadings. It is a life energised by a profound trust in the possibility of divine guidance and by the experience of being loved as one of God's children; by the practice of quiet, patient waiting on the divine and by the experience of quietness as restorative and sustaining. It is a life capable of expressing love for others and joy in the created world because it is nourished by experiencing love and joy.

I believe the spiritual life challenges evil, confronts oppression and shares in the sufferings of others. But it is not so submerged in what it works against that it becomes like what it opposes. It is a life lived in harmony and balance because it is capable of being continually renewed and energised by hope for the future, by affectionate goodwill toward others, and by affectionate goodwill toward the self.

There is undoubtedly much more to the spiritual life, but if we could live merely in what my working definitions promise, we could probably be fairly relaxed about waiting to find out what else the spiritual life offered. Let no one reading my words be deceived that, because I can say what I believe the spiritual life is like, my own life is lived that way.

Nourish, Nurture, Nurse: These three words can be used interchangeably to speak about caregiving for others or bringing up the young: 'nourish', 'nurture', and 'nurse'. As English dictionaries customarily distinguish among these words, nourish emphasises providing whatever is needful for physical development, nurture suggests tenderness and solicitude in training the minds and manners of the young, and nurse describes activities as various as breast-feeding a baby and helping someone regain health. These three words speak powerfully about how human beings sustain themselves and one another.

To speak of being nourished reminds us that all living things get hungry and have to be fed regularly – several times a day for babies and young children – not just when the impulse occurs to us or when we find the time. To be well nourished means taking regular care for our need for food. The word also reminds us that living creatures have to be fed both what is good for them and what conduces to good health. 'Which of you, if your child asked for bread, would feed it a stone?' Many things will fill us which do not nourish us. Sustaining food is nourishing food.

Nourish also reminds us that being fed in a healthy way depends not only on the food we take in but also on the habits we have developed for eating and caring for the body. Food must be converted to muscle and energy and activity, and we must exercise as well as eat. We have to keep remembering that crash diets do not work in bringing weight down, for example, and that moderation is as important in exercise as it is in eating. At its simplest level of meaning, to nourish means to provide the food which sustains life and fuels our being and our activities.

The metaphorical meanings of these words take on added significance in the light of a new way of understanding the meaning of the word 'education' which has been offered by William Oats, the long time head of the Hobart Friends School in Tasmania, Australia. William Oats challenges the traditional understanding, which has taken the word to mean either drawing things out of a student or leading things into the student's mind. If that were correct, he argues, the word would come down to us as e-duction, (ex and duco, I lead out, or, in) and would be similar to words like 'deduction' or 'induction'.

Instead, he suggests, the word comes from educare, which means to nurse. To nurture a student in learning is not only to provide information and ideas which might be instructive to him or her, it is also to try to inculcate habits of study, which will make it possible for the student to comprehend or digest information, and habits of thought, which enable the student to think critically, independently and, in time, creatively. The teaching-learning process, which is one of the things which helps define what it is to be human, resting on relationships suggested by the inter-connected words nursing, nourishing, nurturing.

We have natural aptitudes and longings for the spiritual life, just as we have for walking and talking, but in each case the natural aptitudes and longings can only be fully realised in the caring support of others. That process of encouragement and nurture is the teaching-learning process, education.

Sources of Spiritual Nourishment

In what follows, I will talk about only five sources of spiritual nourishment which I have known as among the chief sustainers of my life:

    the companionship of other seekers,
    the pleasures of solitude,

the satisfactions of obedience,
the support of prayer and worship,
the gifts of joy.

Each of these has been the subject of profound spiritual writing across the ages. I cannot add to that body of wisdom. I can only write of my hopes, convictions and aspirations. I can offer some of the hints and glimpses of that life which I have received, and which help carry me along in my desire to live it more fully. If I can speak with any authority, it is of what nourishes my life and what drains it of spiritual vitality. Perhaps, in what I say of my own life, others may find confirmation of their own experiences.

Solitude and Companionship

Though the uses of solitude and the search for spiritual companions are different, and need to be examined separately, there are good reasons, at first, to think of their interplay. We need both solitude and companionship, and when our spiritual health is best we know how to receive each with whole heart. When we are not in good health, we spoil each by our impatience for the other. Many of us think we would love to have more solitude in life than we have at present. 'You Quakers,' say some of our acquaintances, 'how lucky you are to be so at home in silence and solitude. If only I had more times of simply being by myself, more times of extended quiet, how much more balanced my life could be.' It does not take a lot of experience with long stretches of silence and solitude, however, before we recognize that they are hard to use well. How soon, in the solitary car ride, before one turns on the radio or the tape-deck? That is to avoid dozing off, of course, and perhaps the automobile is not the wisest place to begin learning the uses of solitude. The story is told of Henry Cadbury that he found himself thinking of a wonderful complex scholarly question as he was driving through a particularly treacherous traffic bottleneck and had to tell himself firmly that that was the wrong time to be thinking about such a question. But we turn the radio or tape-deck on, in the car, as at home, because being alone with ourselves can be difficult. Many spiritual traditions picture the encounter with the Divine as occurring primarily in solitary places like the mountain or the desert, places of often painful testing in preparation for the encounter. Some of the most difficult disciplines of the spiritual life are connected with waiting: waiting to be led, for ways to open, to be given words to say, for the strength to take next steps. Solitude sounds so inviting, but loneliness never is.

Finding Companionship

Even in the most rigorous silence and solitude, in the lives of the cloistered religious, or hermits given over to the practice of interior prayer, the search for God's will is also the search for companionship. Certainly it is a search for the companionship of God, but it also seeks out those companions in the search whose struggles illuminate our own, whose discoveries give us the courage to persist, and whose witness clarifies and sustains our own. What is devotional reading if not a way to find and enter into conversation with a true companion in the search? What is reading liturgy, or singing psalms and hymns, if not another way to cherish our companions? 'There is a spiritual community binding together the living and the dead, the good, the brave, and the wise, of all ages,' says William Wordsworth. 'We would not be rejected from this community; and therefore do we hope.' Among the best ways we use solitude and silence is to invite into our company, and give our attention to, those other witnesses who enlarge the boundaries of possibility for us, who act as reality checks, confirmation and examples for us.

It is a great blessing to have such companions in our daily lives, especially if we can call them on the phone, see them in meeting, get together for meals, exchange baby-sitting with them. Best of all is to share family life and the raising of children with them. But we can also have a larger community of such companions, those we know only through the accounts of their lives or through the words they have left us. I want to dwell on that latter kind of companionship, because I want to consider especially the nourishment that can come from two particular sources: the words of those with whom we agree, who seem to speak to our experiences, beliefs and opinions with great clarity; and the words of those with whom we disagree, who speak of other experiences and beliefs than ours, sometimes truly alien experiences and beliefs, with such genuineness and clarity that we are grateful for their witness, even when it challenges our own.

I especially want to suggest that we impoverish ourselves spiritually when we close ourselves off too quickly from the witnesses with whom we disagree, or when, to appropriate their words for our own beliefs, we translate or transpose what they say into the words and ideas with which we are already comfortable. The pleasure of companionship with those whose words closely fit our own experiences hardly needs explanation, but it deserves at least some celebration. Each of us has known the wonder and delight of having our thoughts, hopes and experiences given back to us by another, perhaps someone of another time or place. In an instant our doubts and our loneliness are relieved. They know what I am going through; they have also experienced what is happening to me. I am not all alone, nor am I crazy to believe as I do. There is at least one other voice which confirms my understanding of reality, and if I can trust that other voice, I will be able to trust my inner voice, as well.

Such companionship is food and drink to our spiritual lives. But it also has its dangers. Being agreed with is not necessarily evidence that I am on the right track. My new acquaintances who persuade me that I am not crazy could also be crazy. If I depend only on the evidence of the like-minded, I may waste my spirit in self-justification, self-aggrandisement. I may also become stale, bored and boring in my spiritual life. Years ago a book appeared called *The Power of Negative Thinking*[1], which I loved simply for its title. It had as an epigraph a made-up quotation from Voltaire: 'I agree with everything you say, so shut up!' Sometimes, even in meeting, I find that phrase recurring to me, warning me that I am spending too much of my time with the spiritually comfortable.

That is why the other kind of companionship is so valuable, the companionship of the sincere adversary, the opponent who operates faithfully from a different set of convictions, and whose life bears good fruit. What I have in mind is what happens when we discover that there is no way that we can make our different words mean the same thing, without violating one another's integrity, yet in our separateness we share goodwill toward one another, a trust that we are each right to go our different ways. Such encounters with difference confirm each of us, at the same time confirming that we live in a world where profound differences are significant.

Anyone middle-aged or older in this society will recall how, when we were young, many people of good will were trying to improve what was then called race relations by a strategy of minimising or ignoring racial differences between people. Because the larger society used racial differences invidiously, as the justification for oppression, one would hear sensitive people say, in reaction, 'I never notice what race another person is,' or 'I forgot to notice whether she was black or white.' Parents would try to train themselves and their children to ignore or suppress awareness of racial differences. In those days, when segregation in housing, public accommodations, restaurants, recreational facilities and the like was common everywhere, the foundation stone of those working for integration was to ignore or forget our racial or ethnic differences, except for the occasional ethnically balanced banquet or evening of folk dances from around the world. Let us treat those differences as trivial surface qualities, such sensitive people said, and look beneath the surface, where we are all essentially alike.

When, some years later, Black Consciousness became a powerful liberating force in this society, we had to face that what such forgetting of difference had meant was that some white folks had, truly out of the goodness, though not the wisdom, of their hearts, pretended that their black acquaintances were honorary whites. Denying that the differences between people were important meant denying that our individual identities were important. But what is on the surface is also part of what is in the depths of our being, and it too deserves to be celebrated.

Can African-Americans and Caucasian-Americans become spiritual companions of one another? Can African, Asian and European people be spiritual companions of one another? We know that such companionships, when they occur, can be wonderfully rich, but we also know that they are far more complex to achieve, and frequently require far more heart-sorrow, than we might once have thought. Before we reach such companionship, we have to hear, and say, words which stress profound, sometimes irreconcilable differences. We have to hear hard sayings about ourselves, in silence, neither defending ourselves nor evading what is said by eager self-recrimination. We have to listen carefully to how the other person describes her or his experience, even the person's experience of us, and leave it in that person's own words. We may not appropriate the words to our own experience 'nor translate them into language which is more familiar or comfortable to us. We must learn to be cautious about beginning sentences with 'what I hear you saying is...' or 'in other words...'

The first and most difficult step toward finding spiritual companionship with the other is to acknowledge the otherness with respect. Can an orthodox Conservative Jew and a devout Evangelical Christian become spiritual companions to one another? What they have which is most valuable to one another, their deepest commitments, is also what would separate them most completely. Conservative Jews await the Messiah and live according to the laws which God has ordained. That is their part in preparing for the Messiah. Christians are absolutely convinced that the Messiah has come, in the person of Jesus Christ, and live their lives in the fullest devotion to that conviction. They believe that their part in preparing for the future is to live a life freed from all the laws their Jewish companions try to follow scrupulously.

If we assume that the only way two such people can be spiritual companions is if they agree to avoid all acknowledgement of their differences, or find some level of abstraction which makes the differences look small, we trivialise the lives of both, for their actions and motives, the very textures of their lives, are created by what they believe. And much of what each believes will be simply untranslatable and unassimilable into the other's language.

Think how much more diffficult, even tormented, a process it has become in our time to find true spiritual companionship, the companionship of equals, between women and men. How much see-sawing back and forth we must do, from treating each other as symbol, to knowing each other as individual, to knowing each other simultaneously as individual and symbol, this man and all men, this woman and all women. How many knots we must untie from our pasts, from all the bad encounters we have had with the other, represented now as either man or woman. But think, as well, how much more rewarding that companionship can be, when we each have had to see the world through the other's perspective and treat it with respect. How rewarding it is to work at such a companionship, knowing it as a mutual, reciprocal process.

For many of us, the experience of finding spiritual companionship among people profoundly different from us is a joyful one. The greater the difference, the more careful we are to treat our companions with respect. What is far harder, for many of us, is listening respectfully to, and finding the spark of truth in, those who are in our immediate family. If one is a religious liberal, which is easier to imagine finding companionship with – the Buddhist or the evangelical Christian? The unbeliever, or the fundamentalist Christian? If one is an evangelical Quaker, how easy is it to listen respectfully to the liberal Quaker who says 'there is that of God in everyone'? We have deep respect for the images and practices of Native American spirituality. We have deep respect for the languages in which Hinduism or Buddhism express their commitments. If we met Martians who expressed religious convictions, we would probably be prepared to respect them most of all – for the slighter the acquaintance the easier it is for people of a particular kind of good will to feel respect for others. But for our fellow Quakers of a different tradition, or perhaps for people who speak in traditional Christian language, who needs to listen? Who needs to leave their words in their traditional form? Those are just my idiot cousins talking.

Someone has propounded the riddle: Why are Quakers such poor singers? The answer is, because they are always reading ahead to see if they agree with the words. Like most jokes, that has only a part of the truth in it. And of course there are good reasons to want the words we sing, particularly in worship, to have as much integrity as the words we say. But there are at least two integrities to consider here: my integrity, as I sing or speak the words of another, and the integrity of that other, another person, another tradition, out of which the formulation came. I do not make words my own simply by appropriating them from another and editing them to my own satisfaction. We seem to understand that instinctively with some material. Many of us find ourselves able to sing the original words of African-American spirituals, and perhaps some old Gospel hymns, without feeling compromised, even if some of the words do not express our own experience in the ways we find comfortable. Perhaps we sing those songs as we find them because we know that, at that moment, we are honouring someone else's deepest spiritual experiences, expressing our solidarity with those voices whose songs these are. Perhaps there are some songs and prayers which do not have to be reshaped or updated to fit our orthodoxy. Something about their integrity challenges us, makes them available to us as enlargements of our own language and imagery. Perhaps they show us that our language is thinner than it might be.

Certainly there are times when we must reshape a text from the past, as the only way to make it our own, but perhaps we do that more quickly than we need to, eliminating pronouns or images which differ from our preferred ones before we have found out what they have to say to us. Each text has its own horizon, and we learn most from reading when we let our own horizon line be compared with the horizon line of another, perhaps to find a new horizon line which best incorporates both.

Martin Buber speaks of humans trying to communicate with one another from different faith-perspectives in a lovely image: I stand in the doorway of my faith and greet others standing in the doorways of their faiths. The image reminds us that there is a space in between, which marks our separations but is also public space where all are free to meet and address one another. I may not presume to stand in the doorway of another's faith; I must wait for an invitation to enter. If I enter, it must be as a respectful seeker, not as a tourist sneering at what is unfamiliar. If I stand in my own doorway, I greet others, perhaps with some heart-sorrow that we must maintain some separations because our understanding, experience and integrity require that we stand where we are, but always with good will and gratitude for their witness.

The poet Robert Bly quotes a haiku by Basho[2]:

The morning glory –
Another thing
that will never be my friend.

Commenting on the poem Bly says that we feel separated when we first realise that the natural world may not need us, but then we feel a sense of joy to realise that each thing has its own integrity, independent of us. Not everything has to include us, in order to be valuable or to have its own integrity. I want to suggest that, for many of us, the first task when hearing words which do not agree with us, which express things which trouble us or which we think we have outgrown, is not to stop listening and not to substitute our own words, but to listen harder to what the other person is trying to say. We may find something whose world, in Robert Bly's words, 'is complete without us.' We stand in our own doorway and greet the other standing in his/hers. Something which speaks to our condition may not be saying what we want to hear. When we listen this way, to what is alien to us and may have no particular intention to include us, we may find the spiritual companionship of the adversary and the critic. That may ultimately be more valuable to us than the isolation which comes from hearing only our own voices, or their echoes, again and again.

The Pleasures of Solitude

Rabbi Moshe Leib said: "a human being who has not a single hour for his (her) own every day is not a human being." What a hard saying this seems to be. What can be more human than to give up one's own hour to the needs of others? What should we be called – most of the people I know and work with – who cannot find that hour a day because we give other people priority over our inner needs? What are we being blamed for? But perhaps this is more a warning than a hard saying. In place of an assertion, we can turn Rabbi Moshe Leib's saying into questions:

> You who pour your humanity out for others unstintingly, and never give yourselves the time to replenish it, what will you be like when you have poured out everything you have?
> You who draw on the resources of your inner lives to care for, comfort and teach others, what will you have to give, if you do not refresh your inner lives?
> When you have nothing to give, what will you give those who come to you in need?
> You, to whom others come asking for bread, what will you do when you have nothing but stones to offer?
> Are you so sure of your humanity, your inner resources, that you can take them for granted?

Perhaps even the Rabbi's hard saying is not condemnation of those who cannot find the hour, but a diagnosis of what will happen if they never do so. We are used to people who claim they are barely human without the first cup of coffee in the morning, or even the first cigarette; should we be surprised that time of our own is also essential for us to be human? One of the exercises in writing for refreshment which Margaret Lacey has devised invites people to imagine creating the perfect 'room of their own'. People do this exercise with great delight. Some imagine large open spaces high on a wooded mountain top, with separate areas for reading, painting, listening to music, entertaining friends. Others wish for small spaces dedicated to only a single activity. People fantasise about being in the woods, on a lake or the seashore, in the mountains, and some of us want our rooms simultaneously in all those locations! (This is an invitation to imagine, after all.) This writing exercise makes us aware of a variety of needs. Some, especially primary care-givers of young children, may feel what is most lacking in their lives is a combination of stimulating activity and time to enjoy it. For them, a meal where they don't have to cut someone's food is a great treat. They want both companionship which will enrich the inner life and the space to enjoy it. People whose lives are shaped primarily by the service they give others often write of rooms full of energy and resources, welcoming to soul-mates. For others, life may have too much stimulation, too many exciting demands, maybe even too many rooms in which to work. A work-life full of enough deadlines, crises and triumphs, lunches with the guys, can make one forget that the soul is hungry. For such people – and I am one of them – their ideal rooms are spare, empty of everything but a table, two chairs, paper and pens. They only want one person at a time to visit, and then only by invitation. For a fortunate few, the room they describe is already theirs, but for most of us it represents fulfilment of something we find in short supply in our lives: time alone, time under our own control, silence and solitude in which we can find refreshment and creativity. The psychologist Anthony Storr calls solitude The Return to the Self[3]: 'Learning, thinking, innovation, and maintaining contact with one's inner world are all facilitated by solitude.'

We do not need to be persuaded that time for ourselves is beneficial, any more than we need to hear many messages on silence in a meeting for worship. What we need is the thing itself though this perhaps does mean, in practice, persuading ourselves (and informing others) that our need deserves priority over other demands on us, that it is not merely self-indulgent to give ourselves time, space, solitude and silence.

But an hour a day? Be serious. I can't get up any earlier, or go to bed any later; there is only an hour to prepare for the next day after the children are in bed; I can't add one more thing to my life. Exactly, if time for oneself is one more bur-den, something which can never take the place of any other claim on our time, we will never find it. Therein lies the huge chasm between the obligation in the Rabbi's hard saying and the invitation to build 'a room of one's own'. It is the reason to think of the pleasures of solitude, not only the nourishment but also the refreshment of time for oneself.

If it cannot be an hour a day, what can it be? As with any good nutritional or exercise programme, we have to start small and simply, respecting our limits and being kind to ourselves. We build our room slowly, so that we may be at home in it when it is finished. For me, the room gets built in very small increments, fifteen or twenty concentrated minutes at a time, once or twice a day, by a mixture of three meditative activities: reading, writing and drawing.

Reading and Writing

A colleague recently told me he was no longer sure he knew how to read for pleasure, not because his work is not satisfying but because, as a teacher of literature, he always feels on duty when reading. Like my colleague, I read almost all the time with pen in hand, to underline, to write notes in the margins, to analyse and make judgements on what I am reading. It is the best work in the world, but it is work, and it does not always feed the inner life. The book I put on a reading list because I love it may not be the right book to feed me when I am preparing it for class discussion. Teachers too resist the assigned work, even when they assigned it.

Reading to feed my inner life does not require covering vast numbers of pages, nor going at great speed. On the contrary, part of its pleasure is that there is no hurry. I may linger over the work as long as I want – in small bits of time, over weeks and months, not in marathon sitting sessions. When I teach *Middlemarch*, I am always trying to squeeze it into two weeks of the term. When I read it for myself, I go slowly, re-acclimatising myself to that roomy world of simple and complex moral choices, of human kindness and cruelties, of generations of people attached to the land. I live in *Middlemarch*, even while I go on living in my daily world and the worlds of the books I am teaching. I live more happily in each of those worlds, care more for other people, when I can return every day or so for a little taste of *Middlemarch*.

That is one kind of reading for refreshment which I value. Another is the concentrated attention on very brief works – the paragraph or two of a Hassidic tale, the psalm, the lyrical poem, the parable. Often such works are short enough that I

can virtually memorise them in ten or fifteen minutes of concentration. Then I carry them around with me, enjoying their
resonance of sound and image and idea. They become like a
melody in my mind's ear, to which I tune my day, a tempo for
my activity. This kind of reading, very much like the *Lectio Divina*
of Christian meditation, is open-ended, imaginative, freed of
most of the responsibilities which I carry into my professional
and scholarly reading. Denis de Rougement speaks of works
of art as traps for meditation, and I read these brief works,
sometimes with intense concentration, at other times in a
relaxed, free-flowing way, to let them come to me on their
own terms, to trap me into meditation. It is like being able to
retire to my own room, with the company of my choice, when
I have a few minutes. So Rilke can speak to me[4]:

> When everything we create is far in spirit from the
> festive, in the midst of our turbulent days let us think
> of what festivals were.

And even on an unfestive day, remembering and celebrating
what has been and can be again, for brief moments I can create
the festive and suffuse the ordinary with its promise.

Most of my writing is to somebody else's specifications: a
consultant's report, a letter of recommendation, memos,
speeches, lectures, articles. The work is mine, and I am grateful
for it; it grows out of what I want to do, and I can grow in
doing it; yet, as with books I assign, the writing I do is not
always an immediate source of refreshment to me. Often it is
hard, plodding effort to find what I need to say and to make it
accessible to my audience, and I only know that I am drained
by the effort to get things right. It will feed me in time,
perhaps, but not when I am doing it. For daily nourishment, I

need other kinds of writing as well.

I once requested, as a Christmas gift, a year's membership in a health club; I went once and never again. Keeping a journal is, for me, like taking out a membership in a health club, an investment I cannot keep up. (This was true until 1994, when I had a heart attack. Since then, I have been going regularly to a gym, helped greatly by the fact that my daughter and son go with me. Claiming the necessary time from all the other demands remains a struggle.) I have never been successful at keeping a journal – though I urge it on many of my students as a good idea. When I have tried, the journal becomes so enticing that I hurl myself into it, writing page after page, hour after hour, for a few days or weeks. What I write is excessively introspective, like the first letters home from college or the poems one writes in airports or motels. Then I find I cannot afford this much time for myself, so I give less and less time to the journal until one day I realise that I have not written in it for months and the few enormous entries look outlandish and obsessive standing all alone.

I cannot keep a promise to myself to write an hour a day just for myself. What I can do for myself is brief regular writing, just enough to keep the juices flowing. Sometimes this will take the form of a single page, written as rapidly as possible the first thing in the morning, then put away until the work of a month or so has accumulated, when I can go back to see if anything in those pages is an invitation to write a poem. Often a poem will begin to emerge, over weeks of writing, from a few phrases of these daily scribbles. That gradual accumulation of images and phrases builds up energy so that I can give myself the time to complete whatever has been taking shape. At other times, especially when I have a lot of writing-to-specification to do, I begin each day of writing with some very simple exercise, such as writing five lines of poetry – not attempting to complete a poem but merely inviting the images to emerge as they will. Sometimes, after a few weeks, I will discover the seed of a poem in that writing, but it is not important whether any finished work emerges from such exercises. These are the writing equivalents to those brief, concentrated readings I can do often enough to keep my inner life nourished. They are ways I can claim, not an hour at a time, but fifteen minutes or half an hour of that time which lets me be a human being. They are also brief withdrawals to that room I have made for myself, from which I can emerge with some inward work having been done for my own sake.

Drawing

In *Drawing on the Right Side of the Brain* Betty Edwards[5] tries to help one develop drawing skills by showing how the work can be done by that part of the brain which is best suited for it. A number of other writers have also addressed the value of, in effect, sharing the brain's work more evenly between its two lobes and giving the overworked left side a rest. Betty Edwards describes right-brain activity this way:

> The characteristics of this subjective state are those that artists speak of: a sense of close 'connection' with the work, a sense of timelessness, difficulty in using words or understanding spoken words, a feeling of confidence and lack of anxiety, a sense of close attention to shapes and spaces and forms that remain nameless.

She quotes one of her students: 'I feel excited, but calm – exhilarated, but in full control. It's not exactly happiness; it's more like bliss. I think it's what keeps me coming back and back to painting and drawing.'

I have always wanted to be able to draw, though I realise that I draw poorly. A few years ago, I took a very satisfying drawing course from a colleague, and though my skills remain minimal, drawing itself has come to be an important source of inner refreshment for me. Perhaps drawing has become important to me because I am not accomplished at it, for in nothing else am I so aware of the distinction between the satisfactions of a process and the satisfactions of a finished product. I have not yet drawn anything I can take pride in as a completed work, yet the time spent drawing, even when I am frustrated by how I have muddied or overdrawn a sketch or embarrassed at how badly I capture perspective, gives me pleasure. I leave the experience feeling restored, with a greater sense of ease. The process has helped store something up in me which makes me more able to do my work, though whatever it is that I have received cannot, in the very nature of things, be given to others as drawing.

What refreshes me about even brief times of drawing – say twenty minutes now and again spent sketching a rock from the bowl on my desk – is being invited to look steadily at something and to play with what I see. I celebrate the rock's lines and masses, its shades and colours, as I try to capture its roundness and hardness with nothing more than a few pencils and a sheet of paper. Drawing is free play, the delight in process; it can eventuate in wonderful products, but that is not the only reason to do it. It renews me in some of the same ways that reading and writing do, but I believe it has the further effect of changing how I read and write. One of the occupational hazards of teaching literature is that one will be afraid to write in literary forms. How often I have written a line of poetry which pleased me and, a week later, crossed it out because it reminded me too much of something a favourite writer had written. Drawing has helped reduce that self-consciousness, perhaps because it has made what I write more visual and less abstract, more the outcome of play than of work.

The promises of right-brain activity are heady. Indeed, too heady for some people, who in what would seem to be a stereotypical left-brain approach, try to make a panacea of right-brain activity. Convinced that all the terrible things which humans have created (e.g. linear thinking, rationality, war) come from the left side of the brain, they think that everything wonderful (e.g. organic thinking, intuition, peace) will come if we simply resolve to shift modes; so they take thought, pick up a pencil or paint-brush, and hope to accomplish bliss. But one does not get away from abstractions by trying to draw them, any more than one frees the intuition by thinking unkind thoughts about the rational. The point of these comments about reading, writing and drawing is not to suggest that, if it takes an hour a day to be human, we can streamline that to twenty minutes here and there. That would be like suggesting, as the comedian Stephen Wright has proposed, that one install a microwave fireplace and enjoy a whole evening by the fire in eight minutes.

Most of us would probably be glad to have more time for being alone to practise the arts of solitude which refresh us. But whatever time we find, we can use in ways which can suffuse the rest of our day. When battered by incessant noise, meaningless sounds, we long for perfect silence; yet our souls are not nourished in sense-deprivation, but in time spent in the living companionable silence of nature, where there are always birdsong, the hum of insects, running streams or tides, and the whisper of wind in the trees.

Rilke speaks for many of us when he wishes for that perfect time of stillness, when thought could think the divine completely into itself, when we could, for that moment, possess God completely, then surrender God back into the creation. But Denise Levertov[6], reflecting on those longings, brings us gently and joyfully back down to the everydayness of life:

There will never be that stillness.
Within the pulse of flesh,
in the dust of being, where we trudge,
turning our hungry gaze this way and that,
the wings of the morning
brush through our blood
as cloud-shadows brush the land.
What we desire travels with us.
We must breathe time as fishes breathe water.
God's flight circles us.

If we only think of meaning as something which must be distilled from our daily lives, we will be frustrated and unhappy much of the time. The secret is to find the meaning diffused in our lives, as fishes breathe water, drawing the life-giving oxygen from the medium in which they live and move and have their being.

The Satisfaction of Obedience

Someday I would like to compile an anthology of leadings that didn't seem to go anywhere. Two of the most compelling Quaker examples are reported by George Fox and by John Woolman. Fox reports in his Journal that his first leading in a social concern was to speak to the justices in Mansfield about servants' wages. Going to deliver his message, Fox finds that the justices are being distracted by some fiddlers, so he leaves, planning to return the next morning. When he returns the next day, he is told the justices have left, whereupon Fox is immediately stricken blind. He learns that the justices have gone eight miles, to the next town, and his sight begins to return as he starts running to get there. He arrives and delivers his message about wages and about servants working honestly, which he says is well received by the justices. And that is the end of the story. There is no indication that servants' wages are improved one penny, or that they work any more faithfully, as a result of Fox's following his leading.

Woolman's story builds and builds to an anticlimax, like a shaggy dog story. First, Woolman feels an urging to go to the Barbadoes. As always, he struggles with the leading for a long time before sharing it with his meeting. He then goes through every step of discernment and clearness that the Society of Friends provided, an exceedingly careful, deliberate and slow process. And Woolman is himself a seasoned Friend, very experienced in discernment. At each stage, he is supported in being faithful to his leading. Eventually, he is resigned to go, but then another difficulty arises: he will have to take passage in a ship which is involved in transporting slave-made goods. Woolman wrestles with this problem until he concludes he must pay a larger amount for his passage, lest his trip be sub-sidised by slave labour. With that resolved, he is free to take the next step, which is to leave home and go to Philadelphia, where he will take ship for Barbadoes.

Then, the night before he is to take passage, Woolman realises that God has relieved him of the obligation to go, so he returns home.

The story invites us to ask ourselves what we would have done in Woolman's place. Imagine going back and telling all those Friends who had been working through this massive collection of scruples that you didn't need to go, after all. 'It's all right Friends, God said "never mind".' Today, of course, the plane ticket would be non-refundable and we, or the meeting, would lose all that money. Wouldn't we feel like fools? – Someone who couldn't even read a leading? Wouldn't we be tempted to go anyway, since the ticket was paid for, at great extra effort and cost? What harm would it do? But Woolman follows his leading only as far as it goes, and no farther; and the episode, taken by itself, seems slightly comic. Catch me serving on a clearness committee for him again!

My anthology could contain a number of other strange stories of Quakers led to do inexplicable things, such as walking barefoot through the streets of Lichfield, preaching aloud in the woods to an empty camp, or being led to go to Russia and ending up providing aid for Finland. And, of course, if I went outside the history of the Religious Society of Friends, the examples would multiply. I might include St Francis of Assisi apparently wasting his time rebuilding an abandoned church or Jeremiah buying a plot of land just before the exile he knows is coming.

Perhaps each of us has had some personal experience of knowing we had to do something which would seem foolish if we had to explain to others what we were doing and why. Some of us have discovered our life's work through such inexplicable nudges, which we may have identified only as hunches or intuitions at the time, for fear of claiming too much. But looking back, we know that something stronger was at work: we had been led. Sometimes it is as low-risk as feeling a strong urging to make a phone call because someone has been on our minds. At other times it is writing a letter or sending a contribution or some other act of opening up. How else can I explain knowing that I should make a contribution to this good cause for the first time, when I receive hundreds of well-written solicitations for money, virtually all of them for good causes, in the course of a year? Yet something lifts up this cause to my care, and I act, in some cases then opening myself to a long-term and increasing involvement with the cause. When I am in a big city, I am asked for money by dozens of people every day. I know I can't give money to all of them, just as I know that it is wiser in any case to contribute to organisations working with the homeless. Yet invariably there is someone to whom I feel I must give enough money to be of some practical use. Is this simply to salve my conscience by some kind of gesture? Perhaps. But it is also some other kind of compulsion, some sense that this gesture will be of some immediate help to the person who stands in need before me. 'Leading' seems too elevated a word for so small an act, but I know what I have to do and that I will be troubled if I do not do it.

Sometimes this urging comes as a strong sense that one has to ask another how he or she is feeling, and hearing the answer opens up a large, unexpected area of obligation. Such things have happened many times in my life as a teacher. Perhaps it is the way someone has looked, perhaps there has been no sign I could identify, but I know I need to call or send a note, and then I have opened myself to some new level of association with and responsibility for a student or a colleague.

When such things happen, I experience two kinds of satisfaction: the satisfaction of having been at the right place at the right time, of having asked the right question when it was needed; and the satisfaction of having obeyed the impulse, hunch, leading or command. Most of us have had that feeling – 'I am so glad I asked'. One feels good at having been given an unexpected opportunity; a friendship has begun, or been deepened.

The second kind of satisfaction has been especially important for me, for it is not a matter of having been right in following a hunch, intuition or leading, but of having been faithful. Sometimes much more happens, and I am given a great gift of joy at the fulfilment of some work begun long before. That happened recently, when a former student visited unexpectedly because he wanted to tell me, after twenty-five years, that his life was in good order. 'I wanted you to know that you hadn't wasted your time on me,' he said. I had never thought that I had wasted my time, but neither had I had any sense that my former student's life would be changed by anything I did. To have his visit was a blessing, a finishing off of something for both of us. But twenty-five years earlier, all I had to go on was the satisfaction of knowing I was doing what I could, as I best understood the situation, to meet a need. And that would have been enough, had I never heard from my student again.

The word satisfaction often carries mildly negative associations with it – smugness, being too comfortable or unduly pleased with the self – but I use it deliberately for its literal meaning. To be satisfied means merely that we know something is enough. If my hunger is satisfied, I have had enough, but not too much, to go on. Much of the time, that sense of enough is all we have to go on. We do what we know has to be done, and have no reward other than that sense that we have done what it was given us to do. We are content that we have been obedient. 'For us, there is only the trying. The rest is not our business,' says T S Eliot.[7]

Such experiences of obedience rarely carry with them a great sense of adventure, or a mystical opening, but they are important for the reason that keeping up any healthy habit is important. They keep us in training for more demanding work. So it is with the examples from George Fox and John Woolman cited earlier. Fox realises that he may have lost his first opportunity to be faithful to a leading, and failing this small test could mean not receiving other leadings. A way had been opened, but by mistake he had not taken it. Now he must set off blind and, experiencing literally what most of us have experienced metaphorically, he finds his sight starts to come to him as he goes. It is hardly possible to imagine a better illustration of the phrase 'the way will open'.

And though John Woolman does not go to the Barbadoes, his Journal account shows us that, in preparation for that trip, he has recalled some unfinished, unsatisfactory business of years before, having to do with his being an executor of a Friend's estate and having allowed a slave to continue in servitude. He sets that right, doing what is sufficient to clear or satisfy his conscience, and perhaps that is what all the apparent leading to Barbadoes was about. 'God writes straight with crooked lines,' in the old Portuguese proverb. But as we read on in Woolman's Journal, we discover that he falls seriously ill after the Barbadoes testing. In the depth of that illness he has the powerful vision of being involved in the anonymous grey mass of suffering humanity and learning that John Woolman, the self, was dead. That devastating, yet ultimately liberating, vision seems a preparation for his final journey, the trip to England which ends in his death. Woolman had learned to be satisfied or content that he did not need to go to Barbadoes, as he learned what was enough to clear his conscience as executor of the will. He had remained obedient in the small and even puzzling things, which made him serviceable for the greater callings.

Much more happens in these apparent dead-end leadings, but the more that is added comes, in the first instance, because those called to obedience did as they were led, with no other satisfaction than of having kept faith. It is a great nourishment to the spiritual life to have such satisfaction, to know that, whatever fragmentary leadings one has received, one has tried to be faithful.

The Support of Prayer and Worship

It must seem obvious that prayer and worship can signifi-cantly nourish the spiritual life. When they are alive, they enrich the times of solitude and make the silence resonant. The psychologist D. W. Winnicott speaks of a paradox of human life that 'the capacity to be alone is based on the experience of being alone in the presence of someone, and...without a sufficiency of this experience the capacity to be alone cannot develop.' The person who prays privately, he says, 'feels himself (herself) to be alone in the presence of God'.

What is less obvious, but no less true, is that the spiritual life can be nourished and nurtured by practising prayer and worship even during those stretches of time, sometimes weeks, months and years on end, when the practice seems to produce no fruit. A spiritual life which so emphasises the experiential, the direct encounter with the Divine, as Quakerism does, is especially vulnerable in the dry periods. And most particularly if the periods of greatest richness have been filled with excitement, high energy, confidence in our callings, any diminishing of that kind of reward may bring with it uncertainty and self-laceration.

All the traditional language for reflecting on these times tends to make us blame ourselves for the dry periods. We have ceased doing something right; we have ceased being obedient. Then we begin to think that this is a painful testing from the Divine, a mysterious and perhaps undeserved emptying-out of whatever has sustained us previously. And finally we may decide that we had always been deceived, that group worship has only been the same kind of self-deception, that prayer is merely wishful thinking and talking to oneself. Sometimes we fall back on the self-protection of cynicism and conclude that no one who speaks in meeting is truly led, only self-deceived or exploiting the language of inspiration to deliver his or her own thoughts. Perhaps we still find the silence refreshing, but we expect less and less to emerge from it, and perhaps we even become increasingly impatient with those who interrupt our silence with messages we are convinced are just the ideas of people riding their hobby-horses.

Yet even in those times of dryness, coming to meeting and waiting in the silence can be nourishing. It can be a time for practising good will toward other people, seeing each person who is there, trying to imagine him and her bathed in light, thinking of what one would wish positive for each. It can be a time for attending to those other voices – those we have found useful in the past and those which have always been a challenge for us. Sometimes we discover new spiritual companions in those periods of dryness: people who have persisted courageously when nothing seemed to sustain them. It is a time for persisting in what has been fruitful in the past, a time for keeping faith with whatever it is that has proved to be sustaining in earlier times. People often tell us to have faith when we are in such times of emptiness, but having faith is exactly what we cannot do. At most we can keep faith, in the same way we keep faith with a friendship, or with a promise which is inconvenient but necessary to keep. We keep faith by coming to meeting, by practising whatever form of prayer or meditation has been useful in the past, and by trusting those whose ministry has spoken to us in the past.

What can be nurtured during those times of waiting without response? Patience; humility; kindness to one's companions in the waiting; kindness to oneself; stubbornness in a good cause; the capacity to act without reward, for the sake of the action itself.

Many of these same qualities can be nurtured during those times when prayer feels like talking in a vacuum. I think of the hymn *Spirit of God, Descend upon My Heart*, itself a prayer for that kind of situation:

I ask no dream, no prophet ecstasies,
No sudden rending of the veil of clay,
No angel visitant, no opening skies;
But take the dimness of my soul away.

And the end of another verse says simply '…Teach me the patience of unanswered prayer.'

George Fox tells us that, after his great opening, that Christ Jesus could speak to his condition, his heart 'leaped for joy'. Shortly thereafter, however, he finds himself enduring terrible temptations, during which he discovers that all the horrible things which were to be found outwardly, in the world, are also to be found within, in the hearts of wicked people. Even worse, these temptations make him realise that the same terrible evils live within himself, and he asks God why he should be so afflicted, since he had never been so tempted before. Fox has suffered far worse than dryness, through no fault of his own. Yet fault would have been all the traditional explanations could have offered him. Like Job insisting 'though he slay me, yet will I trust in him, but I will maintain my ways before him', Fox challenges God for an explanation. And God answers that it is needful for Fox to experience all conditions, or he could not speak to all conditions. What is nurtured when we can only pray 'take the dimness of my soul away' or 'teach me the patience of unanswered prayer' is the capacity to speak compassionately, as a fellow-sufferer, to the conditions of people in that same state, and to speak, perhaps, as one who finally finds those prayers are answered. At the end of his account of this experience, Fox records:

And in this I saw the infinite love of God. I saw also that there was an ocean of darkness and death, but an infinite ocean of light and love, which flowed over the ocean of darkness. And in that also I saw the infinite love of God; and I had great openings.

Prayer – the focusing of attention on the Divine, in acts of praise and gratitude, supplication, confession, petition on behalf of others, even challenge – and worship – of which prayer is a part, but which also includes listening, waiting for ministry, ministering when led to do so – both prayer and worship may lead us from the ocean of darkness and death up to the infinite ocean of light and love. But they do not nourish us only when or if we reach that point. They also feed us in tenderness and solicitude while we are struggling in the ocean of darkness. They would be of no value to us if they could only feed us once we were safely in the light.

The Gifts of Joy

The deepest, most glorious experiences in our lives, we can never describe, only circumscribe. The more they mean to us, the more we have to resort to similitudes, the more we have to keep asking our listeners, 'do you know what I mean?' We have to speak in indirection, in what T S Eliot calls 'hints and guesses, hints followed by guesses'.[8] Even the words which stand in for these experiences are short: monosyllables like 'love', 'grace', 'joy'. But those events which transform and humanise us beg to be shared with others, however clumsily. So, because they nourish my life so richly, I want to talk about the gifts of joy.

One of the things we know about joy is that we can't make it happen. Though it can come to us from many directions and many sources, it always comes on its own terms. Prosaic dictionaries speak of joy as high pleasure, gladness, delight, happiness. Celebrating it in its absence, in the poem *Dejection*[9],

Samuel Taylor Coleridge calls joy 'this strong music in the soul', 'a light, a glory, a fair luminous cloud', 'a beautiful and beauty-making power.' Joy is a gift, one we cannot will for ourselves, nor even for others.

When it comes, we are, in Wordsworth's wonderful phrase, 'surprised by joy'. Yet, if Coleridge understands what it has been for him, joy is not only an event or occasion which comes to us from outside, it already resides in the soul, waiting to greet and affirm the experience which occasions our delight. If so, joy may be at least two gifts: one, the occasion over which we have no control; and the other, the capacity to be joyful, which we may be able to learn and practise. The first is a gift of joy; the second is a gift for joy. That second gift may be like the gift of a good ear in music or the capacity to work with young children, native abilities which can be developed into true skills. Nothing is joyful, if we cannot receive and welcome it as joy when it comes. Though we cannot will joy, we can let joy be our teacher. Perhaps that is how we can develop the gift of joy as the 'strong music of the soul'. We can let joy teach us how to practise openness to it, how to trust that we can know it.

Poetry has been one of my most powerful teachers about joy, so I want to share some passages from a very great poem about joy, William Wordsworth's Tintern Abbey[10]. The poem grows from an extended meditation on the poet's immediate past, stimulated by a scene in nature which he is revisiting after five years. Those have been years of turmoil: his great hopes for political and social reform of society have been destroyed; he has been disappointed in his own ethical blindness; his imagination has failed badly when he had 'yielded up moral questions in despair'. That last word is very important: despair, hopelessness, the very opposite of joy. But, with all his inadequacies and disappointments, he has come back to a beloved spot, accompanied by the person who loves and understands him best in the world, his sister. Things seem to be on the mend.

The conditions are right, then, for the poet to reflect on what had anchored him to some hope in the worst of those years. And he finds two such anchors, his memories and his feelings. The memories are of this beloved place, or previous happiness, and of times when life had balance and harmony. His feelings of love, pleasure, connectedness with both the natural and the human world have helped keep him going. When memories and feelings were deadened, so were his imagination and his capacity to face moral questions. For, as Wordsworth discovers, in so many ways our ability to deal with moral questions depends on the health of our imaginations, our capacity to put ourselves in another's situation, to imagine a better future or the hopes of others.

Memories and feelings of unremembered pleasures, the poet says, influence what he calls 'that best portion' of a good person's life, '... little, nameless, unremembered acts / Of kindness and of love'. This seems to describe what I have called the second gift of joy, the ability to receive happiness when it is given. It is touching to consider what those acts are like, which the poet says make up the best portion of a good person's life. They are habitual acts of kindness, unplanned, unselfconscious acts of love. They are little, nameless and unremembered, even to the person who performed them, because we have been allowed to forget self in those moments. We have not been saying to ourselves or to others, 'Look at me. Notice how kind I am? This is typical of me, really.'

And those habitual acts of kindness and love are fuelled by moments of pleasure and joy which are so deeply embedded in us that they too are unremembered. Because of such moments, even far in our past – before we can remember what we remember, Wordsworth says in *The Prelude* – we have a little something to spare from our emotional life, impulses to generosity or loving kindness which come to us because life just feels right at the moment. We draw refreshment from wells we do not know we possess. The heavy and weary weight of the world is lightened, Wordsworth says. We do not turn away from the hard work of living, but for a time the burdens are a bit lighter.

The poem reminds us that joy has a great deal to do with living the here and the now intensely, with trusting that our lives can be knit together so that the moments of pleasure and joy in the past continue to feed us in the present, and with trusting that this present moment, if we can be alive to it, and greet it with hope, can feed us in the future. In another poem, *The Sparrow's Nest*[11], Wordsworth recalls what his sister contributed to his spiritual growth:

> The blessing of my later years
> Was with me when a boy:
> She gave me eyes, she gave me ears;
> And humble cares, and delicate fears;
> A heart, the fountain of sweet tears;
> And love, and thought, and joy.

Joy may come in huge experiences, amazing transformations, but for most of us it is more likely to come in small realisations, small moments of celebration and ease, small moments when we have the energy and impulse for kindness and love. Those moments of balance, harmony and joy come about in part because we have learned simple habits of trust, of receptiveness to the gifts which the everyday can give us. Memory nourishes hope.

From those same sources of nourishment, Wordsworth tells us, can come something even more powerful –

> that serene and blessed mood,
> In which the affections gently lead us on –
> Until, the breath of this corporeal frame
> And even the motion of our human blood
> Almost suspended, we are laid asleep
> In body, and become a living soul;
> While with an eye made quiet by the power
> Of harmony, and the deep power of joy,
> We see into the life of things.

Anyone who has experienced a gathered meeting for worship will recognise its resemblance to what Wordsworth is describing in this passage. The meeting for worship can be a time when our sense of the rightness of things, the gathering up of those recollections of joy, the gathering of those impulses which are so deep that their sources are unremembered – though we know they can be trusted – the gentle leading of our affections, all these bring us to serenity, to that quietness when we become a living soul, waiting patiently, resting in obedience. And we see into the life of things.

It is power which so quiets us: energy, sources of nourishment for the spirit. Wordsworth names the power: the power of harmony and the deep power of joy. One of those is outside us, a quality in the world, or in a human community, which we discern. That is the power of harmony. The other comes from within us, in grateful response to what we discern, in celebration of the harmony we see and feel. That is the power of joy.

It is hard for many of us to trust joy and the power of joy. I am not talking about how we deal with false joys and comforts, I am talking about our propensity to fuel our social and political actions by fear, anxiety, anger, even hatred, because those are the things which we know will keep the energy level high. For many years after we were first married, we subscribed to a monthly political magazine, a longtime favourite with political liberals, particularly liberals of a Quaker kind. We found the magazine's views generally congenial with our own, but over time we found that reading it never gave us a sense of encouragement that others agreed with us. Instead, we began to realise that we rarely read an issue of the magazine without feeling our hopes and energies drained, rather than enhanced. Its editorial stance always seemed to be 'just as we warned, things got worse again last month, thank God'.

We continued subscribing for a longer time simply because we were invigorated by one columnist – as clear-eyed as anyone we knew, as apocalyptic as any, but blessed with a superb sense of humour. His spirit of fun gave us hope. But, as the years went on, more and more issues contained letters complaining that this was no time for making jokes, it was in bad taste to be so funny when the world got worse again last month (thank God). That magazine could never give us any positive hope; it could only feed our fears and angers.

People like us get hundreds of letters each year, appealing for support for good causes. How often does a letter ask for support by saying, 'we are getting somewhere, things are getting better, so keep up your support'? In my experience, rarely. Far more common is the letter which says that things are worse now than at any time in thirty, forty, fifty years, that the plight of every group, every cause, is more desperate now than at any time in recollection. If we give, it is not out of hope but out of desperation, not with the expectation that we can help things to get better but hoping only to postpone the inevitable catastrophe.

Think how often our first impulse, our conditioned response, when presented with anything hopeful, is to look for a dark, terrifying side. Here is a conversation I overheard within the past year. 'Aren't you excited by the new freedom in Eastern Europe?' 'The thing we have to worry about is that all those governments will turn right-wing.' Not a pause for breath; not a missed beat. Don't be fooled by the treacheries of hope. Stick with the tried and true motive for action, fear. Things got worse again last month, thank God.

In Meeting for Worship, a message expressing delight in the joyfulness of our little children must be corrected by a reminder that many children around the world are suffering. In another meeting, a message about finding joy in simple everyday things is answered – there is no other word for it – by a passionate assertion that, while any of our brothers and sisters anywhere around the world is suffering, the Friend speaking will never feel joy. Surely that is too much to promise. It is far more than we can believe God is asking of us. Is that Friend really called to be the last human being on earth to feel joy? What can account for the intensity and pain in such messages, except our fear of a gift for joy?

Of course people are suffering at every moment around the world. Of course the suffering of little children is the most terrible of all. But the happiness of children and the joy of simple things are also real. They have the power to nourish our spirits by reminding us that the purpose of life is to find and increase the joys of life.

There is something in many of us which fears hope and joy, and which especially does not want to hear anyone else being momentarily happy or at peace. We are afraid that people, including ourselves, will stop being dedicated to improving the world and human societies unless they – we – are terrified into working. So of course we need cynical explanations for events, conspiracy, and especially enemies – somebody to hate in the name of love. We have a mind-set which makes us tend to make friends of our enemies and enemies of our neighbours. When it looked, for a split second, as though peace might break out, with the end of the Cold War, two kinds of people seemed to suffer the greatest anxieties – the Pentagon types and the opponent-of-the-Pentagon types. They and we were alike in being afraid to face a world where we might have to change what we had been doing.

We know that fear and anger and hatred are very powerful fuel – sources for human actions, more powerful than the nuclear weaponry they helped create. It is not uranium or plutonium which triggers a nuclear bomb; it is fear or anger or hatred.

But though they are fuel-sources, they can never be sources of nourishment. They cannot feed and enhance life. They are stones we are given when we ask for bread. What can nourish us, encourage us, sustain us, is joy – the capacity to feel it, to welcome it in others, to entrust ourselves to its restoring power.

The poet Denise Levertov is one of the great political activists and spiritual witnesses of our time. Few have written more poignantly of how it feels when the evil of the world blurs the poet's 'caressive sight'. And none have written more powerfully of what it means to cling to joy in the face of all that evil. In her poem-sequence about Julian of Norwich, Denise Levertov describes Julian envisioning the very spirit of evil, and laughing. 'Julian laughing aloud, glad with a most high inward happiness...'

Julian is given a vision of both the absolute of evil and the absolute of good. Like George Fox she knows an ocean of darkness and an infinite ocean of light and love above it. She laughs out of joy, and the poet turns to Julian because she 'clung to joy',

.. clung like an acrobat, by your teeth, fiercely, to a cob-web-thin high-wire, your certainty of infinite mercy.[12]

We must know unhappiness, despair, anger. They are inescapable facts of life, necessary responses to oppression and human suffering. And, in any case, we must know all conditions before we can speak to them. But the way to speak to all conditions is to offer what is healthy and nourishing, and we are nourished by happiness, not unhappiness, by hope, not despair, by love, not anger. We are called to 'walk cheerfully over the world, answering that of God in everyone', and that cheerfulness must not be minimised. It does not mean trivialising human sorrow or human wickedness, or human pain. It does mean reaching down to the deepest reality, the Spirit within which is also the Spirit which sustains the world. And in that deepest reality we find the deep power of joy; we find ways to live so that others can receive the gifts of joy within themselves.

The spiritual life has many sources of nourishment, among them the companionship of other seekers, the pleasures of solitude and silence, keeping faith as we wait for leading, experiencing the confirmation of having followed the leadings we have been given, and times of testing. In each of these, when I know I am being nourished and nurtured, I know something of joy. And there are other times I receive joy – as a gift of serenity, balance, deep happiness, and I know this is food for my spirit now and through the rest of my life. I also know it is not something to clutch to myself but something I am to share. What I know experientially, millions of others have also known. When we share about the spiritual life, let us not be afraid to say what we know. Let us not, above all, be afraid to share the fact of joy, the gifts of joy. Joy is finally the greatest source of nourishment for the spiritual life, because it is God's greatest gift to us.

References

1 *The Power of Negative Thinking*, Deanne Richmond, published by Deanne Richmond,1988.
2 *The Morning Glory: twelve prose poems*, Robert Bly, Kayak Books, San Francisco, 1969.
3 *Solitude*, Anthony Storr, Fontana, 1989.
4 *Rilke, The Sonnets to Orpheus*, translated by Stephen Mitchell, Simon and Schuster, 1985.
5 *Drawing on the Right Side of the Brain*, Betty Edwards, Harper Collins, 1993.
6 *Breathing the Water*, Denise Levertov, New Directions Publishing Corporation, 1987.
7 'The Dry Salvages', *Four Quartets*, T S Eliot, Faber & Faber, 1975
8 'East Coker', *Four Quartets*, T S Eliot, Faber & Faber, 1975.
9 *Collected Works of Samuel Taylor Coleridge*, Princeton University Press, 1993.
10 *Poems of William Wordsworth*, Oxford University Press, 1969.
11 *Poems of William Wordsworth*, Oxford University Press, 1969.
12 *Breathing the Water*, Denise Levertov, New Directions Publishing Corporation, 1987.